AF270408

Dealing with Disorders and Disease

Bipolar Disorder

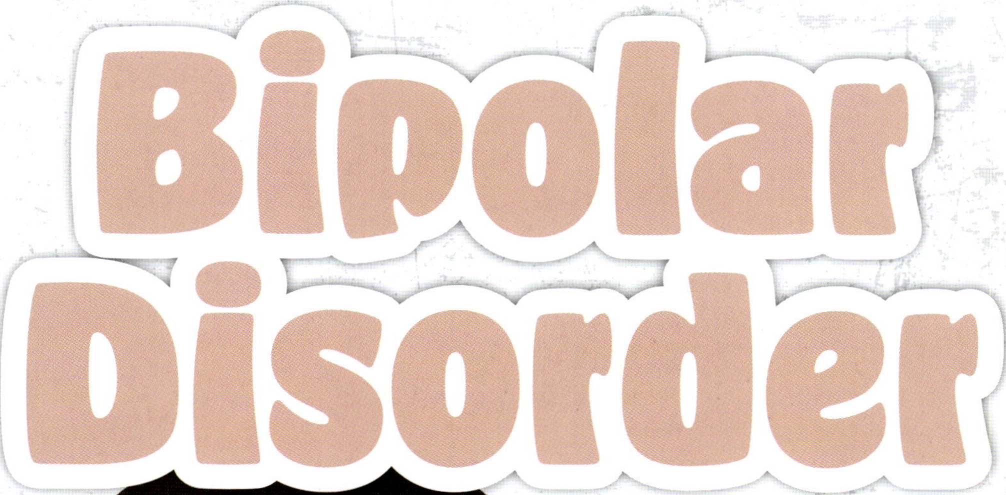

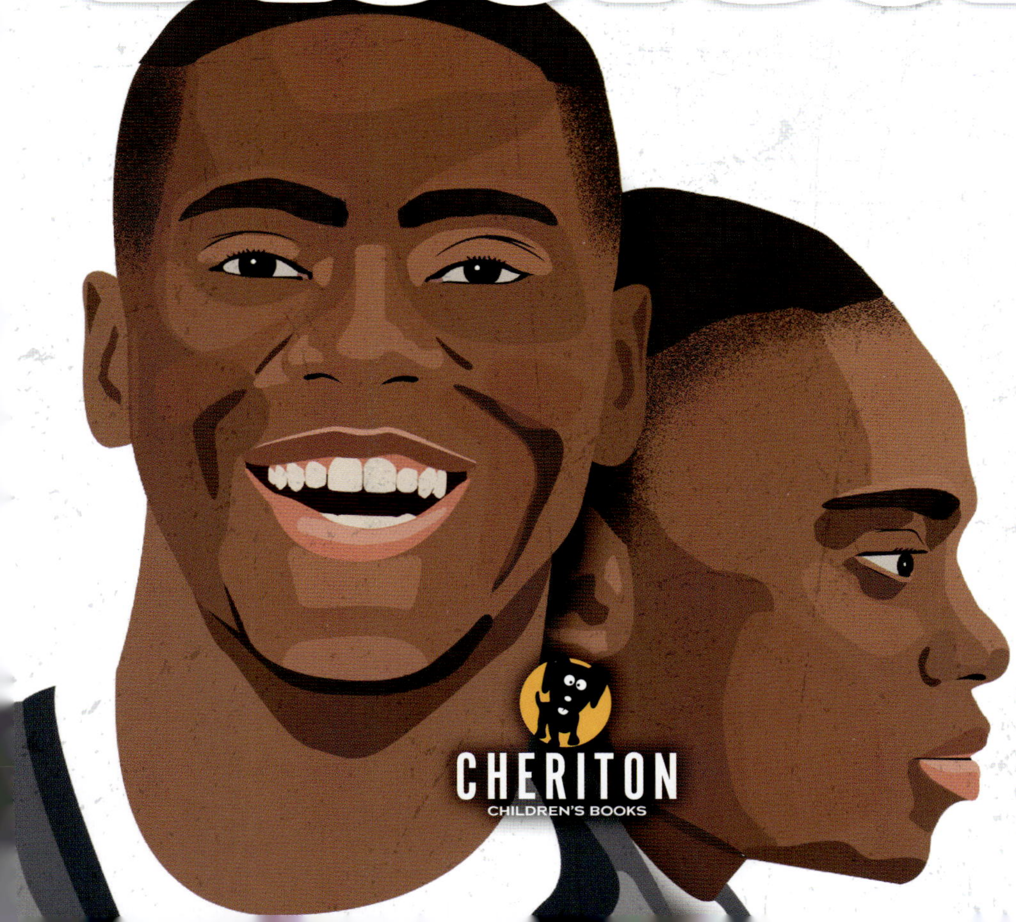

CHERITON
CHILDREN'S BOOKS

Published in 2025 by **Cheriton Children's Books**
1 Bank Drive West, Shrewsbury, Shropshire, SY3 9DJ

Copyright 2025 Cheriton Children's Books

First Edition

Author: Sarah Eason
Designer: Paul Myerscough
Editor: Jennifer Sanderson
Proofreader: Ellie James

Picture credits: Cover illustration by Doodle Press. Inside: p4: Shutterstock/True Touch Lifestyle, p6: Shutterstock/Creative_Bird, p7: Shutterstock/Mapo Japan, p8: Shutterstock/Me Dia, p9: Shutterstock/Michaeljung, p11b: Shutterstock/Mariana Serdynska, p11t: Shutterstock/Fizkes, p12: Shutterstock/Antonio Guillem, p14: Shutterstock/Gorodenkoff, p17b: Shutterstock/Dean Drobot, p17t: Shutterstock/Ground Picture, p18: Shutterstock/Thanakorn.P, p19: Shutterstock/Lopolo, p21b: Shutterstock/Hikrcn, p21t: Shutterstock/Andrei Park, p23: Shutterstock/Jacob Lund, p25: Shutterstock/Fizkes, p26: Shutterstock/Pixelheadphoto/Digitalskillet, p27: Shutterstock/Denis Kuvaev, p28: Shutterstock/Estudi M6, p29: Shutterstock/Evgeniya Grande, p30: Shutterstock/Science Project 101, p32b: Shutterstock/Designua, p32t: Shutterstock/Kateryna Kon, p33: Shutterstock/Yakobchuk Viacheslav, p34: Shutterstock/Yurchanka Siarhei, p35b: Shutterstock/Decade3d/Anatomy Online, p35t: Shutterstock/Nemes Laszlo, p36: Shutterstock/Fizkes, p37: Shutterstock/Oni Abimbola, p38: Shutterstock/GagliardiPhotography, p39: Shutterstock/Prostock Studio, p40: Shutterstock/Ground Picture, p42: Shutterstock/Kmpzzz, p43: Shutterstock/Stock-Asso, p44: Shutterstock/Fizkes, p45: Shutterstock/LightField Studios, p46: Shutterstock/Me Dia, p47: Shutterstock/Peakstock, p48: Shutterstock/RossHelen, p51: Shutterstock/Beach Creatives, p52: Shutterstock/Encierro, p53: Shutterstock/Farknot Architect, p54: Shutterstock/Natee Meepian, p55: Shutterstock/Andrey Popov, p57: Shutterstock/Jacob Lund, p59b: Shutterstock/Daniel Hozvp, 59t: Shutterstock/Fizkes.

Disclaimer: The photographs shown in this book are intended to support the factual content. The publisher notes that the individuals shown in the photographs do not necessarily have the condition/s described in the book.

Printed in China

Please visit our website,
www.cheritonchildrensbooks.com
to see more of our high-quality books.

Contents

Understanding Bipolar Disorder

What puts you in a good mood? It might be a fun time with your friends and family, helping someone out, or experiencing something you have hoped to do for a long time, such as seeing your favorite band. Good moods are great, but it is entirely normal to have bad moods, too. We all get down when something doesn't go our way or if our friends let us down, and we may get worried about something that could happen.

Highs and Lows

Your high and low moods may feel pretty extreme. You might feel so elated or so down that everything else doesn't seem to matter. These powerful moods may even swing from one to another in a short time period. However, some people have swings in mood that are off the scale in comparison. The changes in mood from high to low can totally dominate their lives and make them feel scarily out of control. These people have a condition known as bipolar disorder.

What Is Bipolar Disorder?

Bipolar disorder is a mental health problem or mental illness. This means it is a problem caused by how our brains make us feel and react. Mental health problems range from phobias, such as fear of spaces or spiders, to anxiety, or worrying excessively about things. They vary from bipolar disorder to

schizophrenia, which affects how people feel, think, and act in ways that can be harmful to themselves and others. We can see if someone has a physical illness such as measles or a broken leg, but mental health problems are often less obvious. However, they can make anyone feel just as bad, or worse, than a physical illness. Like some physical illnesses, bipolar disorder can be passed from parents to children through their genes.

You may know someone with bipolar disorder because it is relatively common. About 45 million people around the world have the disorder. In the United States, around 7 million adults live with bipolar disorder. That's about 2.8 percent of the population. In this book, we will look at what causes bipolar, how it can be treated, and what it is like to live with this condition.

Many people still feel they cannot talk about their mental health, despite the fact that conditions such as bipolar disorder are quite common.

In a Mood

People with bipolar disorder experience periods of several days or more when they are stuck in one mood. These periods are called episodes. Depressive episodes are periods when someone feels incredibly low with little energy. Manic episodes are lengthy periods when someone feels incredibly high and bursting with energy. People with bipolar disorder may experience both of these episode types, but also periods with less extreme mania.

Depressive Episodes

A typical depressive episode can last many days or even weeks. People with bipolar disorder experience a range of emotional responses when they are depressed. After all, they are all individuals whose feelings are triggered, or caused or set off, by a wide variety of things. However, during depressive episodes, most people feel:

- Upset and tearful
- Agitated and tense
- Low self-esteem and poor confidence in their abilities and appearance
- Worthlessness
- Guilt
- Lack of enjoyment, even in things they usually like to do
- Exhaustion, or intense tiredness
- Uninterested in food and exercise

During depressive episodes, some people feel like punishing or even harming themselves. Others turn to drugs and alcohol in an attempt to ease their painful feelings.

During a Manic Episode

Manic episodes are totally different from depressive episodes. These episodes last a week or more. People feel a range of sometimes astonishing highs. Someone who is manic is often:

- Incredibly happy, often laughing and telling jokes
- Unusually friendly, or rude or aggressive to others
- Overexcited or agitated
- Distracted, with poor concentration
- Very active and wakeful
- Ready to take risks—they are not only adventurous, but also put themselves in dangerous situations
- Talkative—they may speak a lot and also at high speed, without making much sense
- Prepared to do unusual or inappropriate things

During manic episodes, people may spend a lot of money and make all sorts of promises to do things. Afterward, some people may remember things that happened in an episode and feel unhappy or ashamed about things they have done. Others may remember virtually nothing that happened. People usually feel exhausted after a manic episode.

Understanding Bipolar Disorder

A less severe form of mania is hypomania. Episodes last less than a week and feel more manageable. That is because people can still carry on with normal daily life even if they are feeling incredibly overexcited and full of energy.

Today, more people are aware of mental health conditions and the challenges that come with them.

Naming the Disorder

In the past, bipolar disorder used to be called manic depression because people thought there were always separate episodes of mania and depression. Today, doctors usually avoid describing someone as a manic depressive because they may get hypomanic rather than manic episodes, have overlapping lows and highs, or rarely experience deep depressions. Bipolar disorder is a better term for covering the range of different combinations of moods that different sufferers experience.

Types of Episode

Doctors usually describe five types of bipolar disorder, based on the types of episodes that a person experiences. People will also experience neutral periods between episodes in which they have a normal range of emotions, but no mania, hypomania, or depression. There are five types of episodes.

Bipolar I: This type includes severe episodes of mania and depression, including at least one episode of mania lasting longer than a week.

Bipolar II: This episode features lengthy times of severe depression, often lasting several months, and milder, shorter episodes of hypomania.

Bipolar disorder in children and adolescents can have significant impacts on their lives, including school and college, relationships, and their overall health and quality of life.

Cyclothymia: This type features a blend of brief episodes of both depression and hypomania; episodes are less severe than in Bipolar II, but they occur fairly regularly over two years or more.

Mixed features: This episode includes both manic or hypomanic and depressive symptoms at the same time during the same episodes, or rapidly following.

Rapid cycling: This is a speeded-up form of bipolar disorder in which people experience four or more mood episodes of at least several days each, in a 12-month period; sometimes moods can switch from high to low within a day.

Understanding Bipolar Disorder

Some people have mental problems that share some symptoms with bipolar disorder. For example, someone with obsessive compulsive disorder (OCD) has obsessions such as cleanliness or tidiness; anxiety when things are out of place or possibly dirty; and compulsion, or a strong desire or need, to do things such as clean or tidy up. Some of these symptoms are found in some people's hypomanic episodes. If someone with OCD has periods of deep depression, too, then it is a little like Bipolar II. Some doctors think there is a bipolar spectrum, in which people with bipolar disorder also have other mental conditions. Others think these other conditions are separate, and have different causes and require different treatments.

Bipolar disorder can affect children and teenagers, but is less common than in adults. When it does affect younger people, the two main types of bipolar disorder seen are bipolar I and bipolar II.

Feeling an overwhelming urge to clean the home can be a symptom of a hypomanic episode.

Education and Bipolar Disorder

For a young person with bipolar disorder, going to school can be a challenging and sometimes overwhelming experience. Bipolar disorder can affect many aspects of a young person's life, including their mood, energy levels, cognitive ability, and relationships with other students and school staff.

PROBLEMS WITH FOCUS

Bipolar disorder can impact a young person's ability to concentrate, focus, and retain information, which may affect their academic performance. During a manic or hypomanic episode, someone may experience racing thoughts, feel very impulsive, be easily distracted, and have problems with staying on task during class. During a depressive episode, they may struggle with low energy, reduced motivation, and have problems concentrating. Those extreme emotions and symptoms can affect their schoolwork and make the experience of being at school very stressful and demanding.

LOST SCHOOL DAYS

The symptoms of bipolar disorder, such as fatigue, sleep disturbances, and changes in mood, can lead to periods of time when students cannot go to school. Young people with the condition may miss school days due to difficulties getting out of bed in the morning, overwhelming feelings of sadness or hopelessness, or physical symptoms such as headaches and painful, debilitating stomachaches.

Still a Stigma

Despite improvements in understanding conditions such as bipolar disorder, students may still experience stigma and misconceptions surrounding the condition. Discrimination, bullying, or feeling left out at school by other students makes life at school even more difficult for young people having to manage an already-difficult and upsetting condition.

Although it can also have many benefits, going to school or college can sometimes feel like a struggle for people with bipolar disorder.

ADDING TO THE STRESS

The demands of school, including academic expectations, extracurricular activities, and social pressures, can make symptoms of bipolar disorder even worse. That further adds to the stress of trying to continue their education for people with the condition. Trying to keep on top of schoolwork while dealing with the symptoms of bipolar disorder can feel overwhelming for students, and may lead to feelings of failure. For students going on to college, the change in routine and lifestyle can cause further problems. Dealing with new situations and change can make the symptoms of bipolar disorder worse and trigger episodes. Managing the new demands of college life can be very difficult.

Feeling that they are failing at school just adds to depression and poor self-esteem for students with bipolar disorder.

Dealing with Education

With helpful strategies and a supportive learning environment, children and young people with bipolar disorder can continue their studies and do well. Students affected by the condition may need more support and flexibility than other young people. For that reason, an individual study plan that fits around their needs is often figured out between the student, parents, and teachers to make sure education can continue.

EXTRA SUPPORT AT SCHOOL

Additional support at school for young people with bipolar disorder may include a learning mentor to help them manage their day at school and keep on top of schoolwork. Help with managing workload to avoid too much stress is often needed. Checking in regularly with students to make sure they are managing their work and emotional health is very important. Adjusting expectations and demands as needed makes it much easier for young people with bipolar disorder to stay at school.

Flexibility around attendance helps students with bipolar disorder manage times when their sleep is poor and they are struggling to get to school on time and make it through the school day.

 A plan at school or college for how to manage if a student becomes upset or agitated helps them know that they can deal with the situation if it comes up. For example, having a quiet room where they can go if feeling overwhelmed can reduce stress.

 A supportive, encouraging environment helps people with bipolar disorder learn.

 Having the freedom to take breaks when needed helps students continue with the school day and stops them feeling overwhelmed.

 School staff educated about bipolar disorder can make sure that other students and staff understand the condition too and provide support and empathy for students who suffer from it.

RETURNING TO SCHOOL

Students returning to school after a period of time away will need additional help to join the school system and catch up on lost learning. Teaching staff, healthcare professionals, and parents usually form a plan for return to school with the child or young adult to make sure all the support needed is in place, including extra tuition to help make up lost ground.

CHAPTER 2

Why Do Bipolar Episodes Happen?

During bipolar episodes, people experience a blend of overwhelming changes to their regular mood, sleep patterns, energy, thoughts, and behavior. For some people, episodes come on gradually over several days. For others, the episodes can start with little warning. However, they experience their illness, the root cause of the intense moods in people with bipolar disorder is their brain.

The Control Center

The brain is the headquarters of the nervous system. This is a network of nerves that carry information to and from the rest of the body. Nearly everything we do is controlled by our brains. For example, your brain instructs your muscles to move your limbs, allows you to react to pain, and lets you enjoy music you hear. Each brain contains about 100 billion nerve cells called neurons. They are not just packed together in a big jumble. They are organized into different areas, forming parts with different jobs to do.

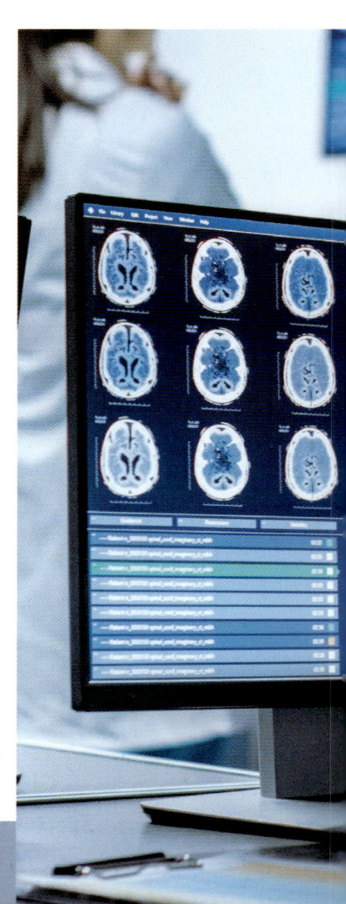

Cerebrum: allows us to respond to the world around us; the front part controls thinking and speaking, and the back part controls vision

Cerebellum: controls coordination of movement, such as keeping balance

Brain stem: controls essential processes that need to happen day and night, such as moving the lungs to breathe and keeping the heart beating

Understanding Bipolar Disorder

Have you ever felt a strong desire to do something daring, such as rock-climbing or singing on stage, even though you are afraid you will fail? The limbic system is a collection of brain parts responsible for all the emotions we feel and things we remember. It makes us feel motivated to do things and experience fear. It is constantly updating new memories of experiences; linking tastes and sights with pleasant memories; and rules of how to behave, including emotional reactions; and moderating feelings of anger. The limbic system also detects if we are thirsty, hungry, getting too hot, or need to sleep. Studies of the brains of people with bipolar disorder have revealed that their limbic systems function differently from those of people without the disorder. This is the brain part that makes a difference in whether someone has the disorder or not.

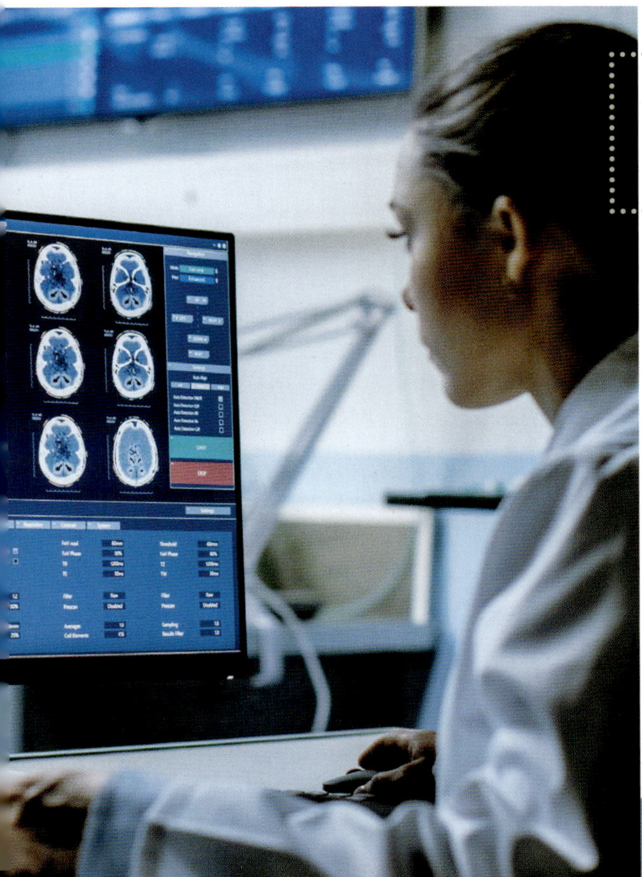

Medical technology is helping us learn more and more about how the brain works.

"Today, our scientific knowledge of the brain is improving all the time, and new discoveries are constantly being made. That improved understanding will help us better understand bipolar disorder in the years ahead."

Mixed Messages

Have you ever played Telephone, when someone whispers a phrase quietly to one person, who whispers it to the next person, and so on? Often, the phrase heard by the last person is very different from what the first person said. In people with bipolar disorder, parts of their limbic system fail to communicate normally with one another. Messages get lost in translation, so they can get misinterpreted. That means that the limbic system has less control of feelings and responses to emotions. To understand how this happens, we need to look at how messages move in the nervous system and brain.

How Nerves Work

We can think of nerves like telephone cables containing bundles of thin wires running through the body. Each wire is a chain of neurons. Bundles of neurons in nerves constantly carry messages to and from different parts of the body. Neurons are special cells with a long part called an axon on one side, and tufty parts called dendrites on the other. Nerve messages move as tiny, very fast bursts of electricity through the axon of one neuron. At the end, they reach a very small gap called a synapse before the start of the dendrites of the next neuron. The messages cross over this synapse using special chemicals that act as messengers. These are called neurotransmitters. The message gets passed on through the chain of neurons in this way.

Understanding Bipolar Disorder

Neurons in the brain do not always make the same neurotransmitter. They make different ones, each with a special meaning. Scientists think that bipolar disorder is caused when one or more of three neurotransmitters called noradrenaline, serotonin, and dopamine are produced in abnormal amounts. Then messages getting to parts of the limbic system become distorted. For example, too little or too much dopamine in the limbic system disrupts normal feelings of pleasure and emotional reward, as well as logical thought patterns. Imbalance of serotonin affects sleepiness, ability to learn and remember, and mood.

Excess serotonin can make us want to sleep for long periods of time. It can also make us disinterested in activities such as learning.

If we imagine a game of Telephone, we can visualize how messages are passed from one neuron to the next to carry them around the body.

First Diagnosis

Bipolar disorder is an illness that people have for life. It can begin in childhood, the teenage years, or when a person is older. Most people are diagnosed with bipolar disorder in early adulthood, usually between the ages of 18 and 30. The reasons people begin to experience episodes are quite varied, but often there are triggers that start them off.

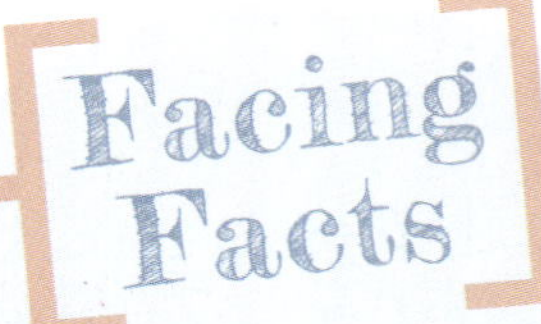

Experiencing bipolar disorder as a young adult is made especially harder because this is often the age at which people are going through important life stages, such as going to college, finding and starting a job, and beginning relationships with partners. All of those stages can trigger symptoms and episodes. Having bipolar disorder can make it more difficult to work, maintain relationships, and find and keep jobs.

Life events such as starting a new job or getting married are exciting, but they can also be stressful.

Under Stress

You probably know someone whose moods and emotions have been thrown into chaos. Perhaps this person broke up with someone, or had deep money worries. Bipolar disorder can be triggered by stressful life events, but also by ongoing stress such as very low self-esteem. Traumatic, or deeply upsetting or disturbing, life-changing events are even more likely to trigger bipolar episodes. These can include being bullied or abused by others, witnessing a horrific event such as a car crash, losing a loved one, or being seriously injured. Low moods, lack of sleep and appetite, and other changes caused by stress and trauma may trigger episodes.

Changes in Hormones

The brain needs chemical messengers to function, but the rest of the body also uses chemicals called hormones to communicate and change. For example, at puberty, the pituitary gland at the base of our brain makes and releases growth hormones, which make us start to grow. The thyroid gland in the neck produces the thyroid hormone. When a thyroid produces unusually low levels of this hormone, a person can experience depression, whereas high levels elevate moods.

Understanding Bipolar Disorder

Some people start to experience bipolar disorder as a result of changing light levels in different seasons. Long, dark winters can trigger depressive episodes, and sunnier, lighter conditions in spring and summer trigger manic or hypomanic episodes. Such changes are the result of the body's biological, or body, clock, which is our internal response to changes in light and dark through every 24-hour period and throughout the year. People with Seasonal Affective Disorder (SAD) also become depressed in winter, but do not experience manic episodes.

In some women, changing hormone levels that occur after giving birth can also trigger bipolar disorder.

Social Connections and Bipolar Disorder

Social support is essential for dealing with the challenges of bipolar disorder. However, people with the condition may struggle to find and keep supportive social networks. Due to the way the disorder affects a person's behavior, forming and maintaining relationships with others can be difficult.

RELATIONSHIP DIFFICULTIES

During manic or hypomanic episodes, people with bipolar disorder may have unusual amounts of energy and behave impulsively. That can lead to behavior that others may find inappropriate, such as shouting, boasting about their achievements, or being extremely irritated with others. At the other end of the scale, during depressive episodes, people may be very quiet and withdrawn, which makes it difficult to connect with others. These extremes of highs and lows can be difficult for friends, family, partners, and coworkers to deal with. As a result, they may avoid being around people with bipolar disorder when they are experiencing episodes, which can isolate the person and make dealing with the disorder even more difficult.

CHALLENGES IN MAKING NEW CONNECTIONS

Forming new relationships can be very difficult for people with bipolar disorder. During highs, they may talk rapidly and about many different, unconnected topics. That can be alarming for people who are not aware of the disorder and its symptoms. People can also have problems understanding social cues when caught up in manic episodes, and be unaware that their behavior is making others feel uncomfortable. People with bipolar disorder may be more argumentative and outspoken during highs, and if people are not aware of the disorder, they can react badly when they come across this type of behavior. During lows, when people may be withdrawn, moody, and uninterested in others, that too can be difficult to accept for people who are unaware that someone has bipolar disorder or do not understand this complex condition.

Because of the stigma that still surrounds bipolar disorder, many people with the condition are fearful of rejection or being labeled "unstable" when meeting people for the first time. For that reason, they may avoid social situations, which can lead to isolation and acute loneliness.

Most people like to have fun, but sometimes when someone is in an extreme episode, their behavior can be very unpredictable.

During low times, people usually become withdrawn and isolate themselves.

Dealing with Social Connections

Forming and maintaining relationships can be challenging for someone with bipolar disorder. However, with understanding and open communication, people with the condition can have good relationships with their family, friends, and other people around them. There are some key strategies that help.

TALKING ABOUT IT

Working on their communication skills helps people with bipolar disorder form new relationships and maintain existing ones. That includes trying to explain what it is like to have the condition to those who may not be aware of it. For someone with bipolar disorder, being open and honest about diagnosis and what it means can relieve worries about how people may react if they witness an episode. For those who do not have the condition, being aware of it can help them react in a more supportive way if an episode does occur.

SETTING BOUNDARIES

It is often important for people with bipolar disorder to set clear boundaries with friends about what they can and cannot handle during mood episodes. For example, it can help to explain that during a low, feelings of sadness can be overwhelming. People may just want a quiet arm around the shoulder and to know that if they want to talk, they can. During a high, very stressful situations make the episode worse, and calm is needed.

FINDING OTHERS

Joining support groups for people with bipolar disorder can provide a friendship circle with others who know exactly what it is like to have the condition. Connecting with people who share similar experiences can reduce feelings of isolation, normalize struggles, and offer practical tips for managing bipolar disorder in daily life.

Being allowed to adapt their social life according to how they feel, and being able to communicate that to friends, helps people manage difficult times.

Understanding that friendships may need to change at times due to the nature of bipolar disorder helps people with the condition and those around them, too.

Being flexible about social plans helps people manage changes in mood and energy levels.

Creating and seeking out inclusive environments makes it possible to form friendships in a safe and supportive place, without fear of judgment.

CHAPTER 3

Genetics and Bipolar Disorder

The chemicals responsible for bipolar disorder are made by cells. Cells are the building blocks of any living thing. The way any cell develops, grows, and functions depends on the instructions found inside it. We call these instructions genes. The role of a gene includes what and how much chemical it produces. Experts believe that the chances of someone developing bipolar disorder depends partly on their genes.

Understanding Genetics

Genes are made up of a substance called deoxyribonucleic acid (DNA). It looks a little like a ladder twisted into a spiral. Each rung of the ladder is made from a particular sequence of chemicals, like a string of letters completing a word. Words in a book of instructions can tell us what to do, just as the genetic code of chemicals in DNA can instruct cells.

Understanding Bipolar Disorder

Only the genes that are actually turned on have any effect on a person. When genes are turned on their instructions become active. Some genes never become active. The gene instructions involved in bipolar disorder are in everyone. But the genes become active in only a few people, who then, unfortunately, go on to develop bipolar disorder.

A Unique Combination

Thousands of genes are twisted and packed tightly into chromosomes inside cells. Each cell in our bodies contains 23 pairs of chromosomes, making 46 altogether. When living things reproduce sexually, one chromosome of each pair from a male joins with another from a female to produce new pairs in their offspring. Each person inherits, or receives from their mother and father, a unique set of chromosomes with its own combination of genes. Particular mixes of genes can make it more likely for a person to develop a particular illness.

We inherit genes from our parents, but the environment we grow up in also plays a part in how we develop.

Facing Facts

Studies have shown that there is a strong link between genetics and bipolar disorder. However, although genetics add to the risk of developing the condition, what happens in a person's environment has a large part to play too. Stress, trauma, using drugs and alcohol, sleep disturbances, and life events can trigger the onset of the disorder and influence how severe it is.

"Bipolar disorder is influenced by both genes and the environment."

Passing on Genes

If your mother has brown eyes and your father has blue eyes, you probably have brown eyes even though you inherited genes for each color. That's because the brown version is dominant, or more powerful, and the blue version is recessive, or can be masked, so it takes a back seat to the brown color form. There are different forms because of changes or mutations in the code of the DNA in the eye color gene. Many medical conditions are caused by mutations in genes.

Brown eyes are passed on to offspring through genes.

Mutating Genes

Mutations can happen when DNA is not copied properly as cells divide during growth and reproduction. They can also happen when people expose themselves to harmful chemicals. For example, chemicals in smoke damage DNA and cause mutations in lung cells causing cancer. Some mutations are neutral and have no effect at all on people, some can be beneficial, and others can cause a disease.

Inherited Conditions

Some genetic diseases, such as cystic fibrosis, can only happen if a child inherits the same mutation from each parent. If a person has cystic fibrosis, their lungs and digestive system become clogged with thick, sticky mucus. If someone inherits just one copy of the cystic fibrosis gene from a parent, they will be a carrier of the condition but won't actually have it. Other genetic diseases, such as Huntington's disease, are inherited if a child gets even one mutated gene.

Not Inherited

Still other genetic diseases, such as Down syndrome, are not actually inherited from a parent. Down syndrome happens when, during the process of reproduction, a child gets an extra copy of chromosome 21. These crucial extra instructions result in a set of developmental changes. Scientists do not think that there is a single mutation making people likely to get bipolar disorder, but instead multiple genes interacting together.

Understanding Bipolar Disorder

Scientists are on the hunt for the genes involved in bipolar disorder. They look for segments of DNA on particular chromosomes that are always inherited by people who have the condition but not by people who do not. These mutations are likely playing their part in the disorder. So far, scientists suspect that parts of chromosomes 12 and 21 are most likely involved. Part of their evidence is that people with Down syndrome rarely develop mania, possibly because the extra copy of the chromosome protects against bipolar disorder.

The extra copy of chromosome that leads to Down syndrome may stop people with the condition developing bipolar disorder.

A Breakthrough in Genetics

It has taken many, many years for scientists to discover that bipolar disorder can be caused by someone's genetic makeup. Key to establishing this has been finding that bipolar disorder often runs in families.

Finding Patterns

Scientists and doctors study populations of people and examine medical records to find patterns of illness so they can figure out causes and treatments. To find out if a disease has genetic causes, they look at patterns of illness in families to estimate their heritability. Heritability is the likelihood that the cause of the illness is due to genes. If one family member has an illness, and there is a higher heritability of the same disease in the family than in people in the general population, then it is likely that genes are playing a significant role in the spread of the condition.

Studying Twins

Many studies of bipolar patients and their relatives have shown that bipolar disorder runs in families. The most convincing genetic data comes from studies of identical twins. Scientists report that if one identical twin has bipolar disorder, the other twin has a 40 to 70 percent chance of developing the condition. The reason studies of twins are important to people researching the spread of disorders and diseases is that twins share some of their genes. Identical twins share all of their genes, whereas non-identical twins share half. It stands to reason that if one identical twin develops the same condition as their twin, then it is likely that genes have had something to do with it. If they have not yet developed the condition, then their chances of doing so are higher than if they were non-identical twins or just regular siblings.

Twins are unique in that they share genetic makeups. Studying both identical and non-identical twins helps scientists understand genetically inherited conditions.

Understanding Bipolar Disorder

Research studies have established the importance of heritability in bipolar disorder. In one study at Johns Hopkins University, researchers discovered that approximately 40 percent of parents or siblings of bipolar patients also had bipolar disorder. In another study at Stanford University, researchers reported that 51 percent of children of people with bipolar disorder had a psychiatric disorder. These included depression and attention deficit hyperactivity disorder (ADHD). Although links between the other psychiatric conditions and bipolar disorder are not clear, such studies support the role of genes in mental illness.

Using Science

In the future, someone living with bipolar disorder may be able to stop it in its tracks. This is possible because scientists have found ways to swap out mutations that cause illnesses and replace them with healthy versions. This process is called gene therapy.

Targeting Genes

Gene therapy targets particular genes in an organism, or living thing. Scientists first carefully identify a mutated section of DNA on a gene that is not functioning properly and might be causing a health problem. They then replace it with a new, functioning gene. The technique of editing, or making changes to, genes was first developed in the 1970s. However, it is only in recent times that improved equipment such as powerful computers and better laboratory techniques for gene editing have been available for scientists to use. Gene therapy is not yet in use to treat bipolar disorder, but it has been successful in treating some illnesses.

Types of Gene Therapy

There are two main types of gene therapy. In one type, DNA is transferred into any cell in an organism that is not a sperm or an egg cell. Then the effects of gene therapy will not be inherited by children of the person being treated. The other type of gene therapy edits genes in sex cells, and therefore changes can be passed on to children from parents.

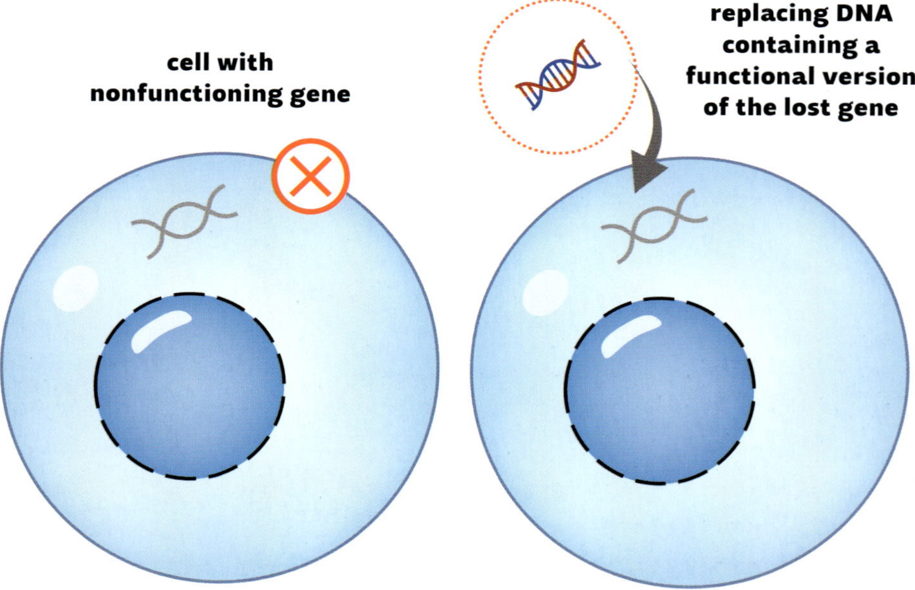

The Human Genome

The first step to gene therapy in humans is pinpointing their genes, where they are located on chromosomes, and exactly what they do. For example, specific genes may cause cells to make particular proteins that have various functions. In 2001, scientists revealed to the world that they had identified nearly 21,000 genes in every human. This was the result of combined efforts of scientists worldwide in looking at the patterns of around 3 billion chemical code units in human chromosomes. It had taken around 10 years of hard work to discover about 90 percent of the total human genome. Work has continued since then, and experts believe they may discover 30,000 genes present in the genome.

Success with Gene Therapy

The first real cures in gene therapy came in treating a rare condition called severe combined immune deficiency (SCID) back in 2000. People born with this disease have to live in a protective plastic bubble because their bodies have no defenses against infections caused by tiny organisms such as bacteria. The treatment edits mutated copies of a gene called adenosine deaminase. In 2016, a safer version of this SCID gene therapy became available. In 2023, another gene therapy treatment was announced.

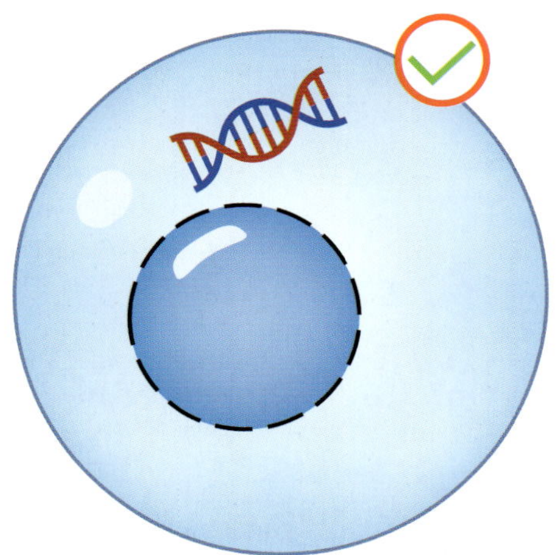

In one method of gene therapy, DNA is replaced in a cell.

Using Cells

The idea of gene editing is fairly simple, but, in reality, it is incredibly difficult to splice a piece of DNA into particular cells in order to change them. Gene therapy uses a person's own cells to treat them, but needs the help of viruses, which are tiny organisms that invade and live in body cells and cause disease.

Infected by a Virus

If you have ever had a cold, then you have been attacked by a virus. Viruses are incredibly small entities (much smaller than bacteria) and have a small amount of DNA in genes protected inside a protein layer. Viruses can only reproduce once they get inside living cells. Once inside, they use energy from the host cell to make hundreds of thousands of copies of their genetic material.

Using Viruses

Scientists can use modified viruses as couriers for sections of DNA. They first remove any of the virus's own genes that cause sicknesses in people. Then they replace them with the normal-functioning gene to be added in the gene therapy procedure. The virus then "infects" human cells with this normal gene, which replaces the mutated one.

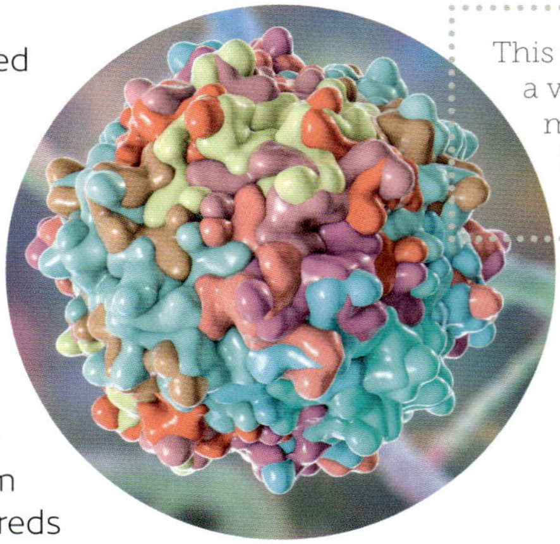

This is a model of a virus. Viruses make gene therapy possible.

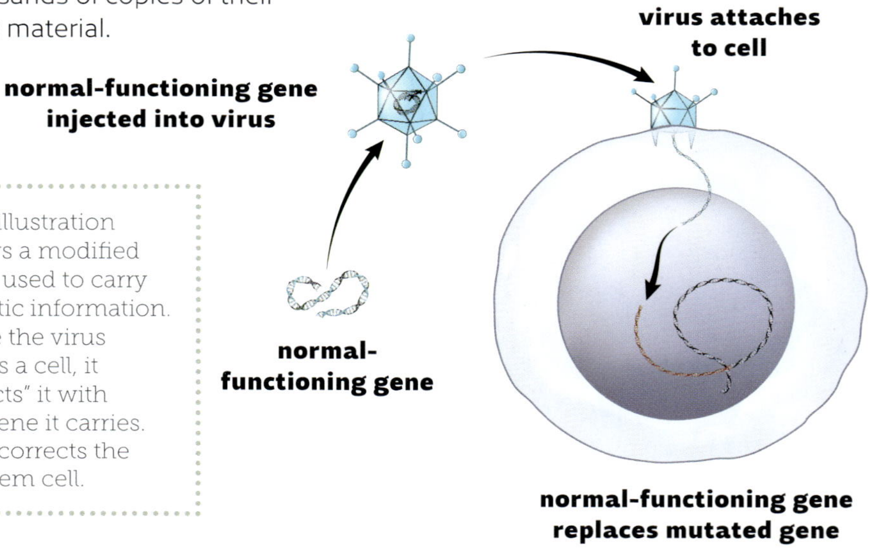

This illustration shows a modified virus used to carry genetic information. Once the virus meets a cell, it "infects" it with the gene it carries. That corrects the problem cell.

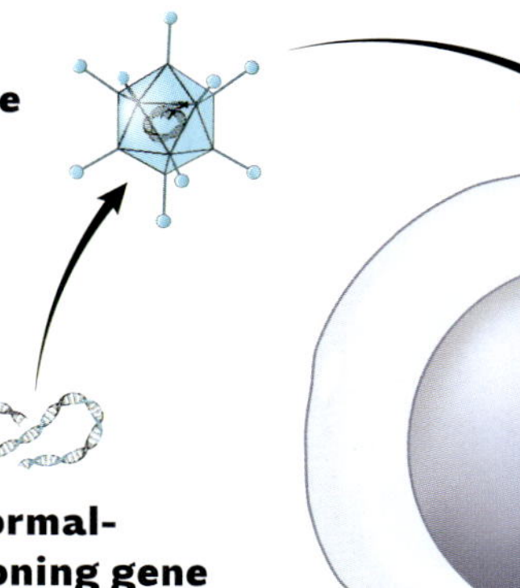

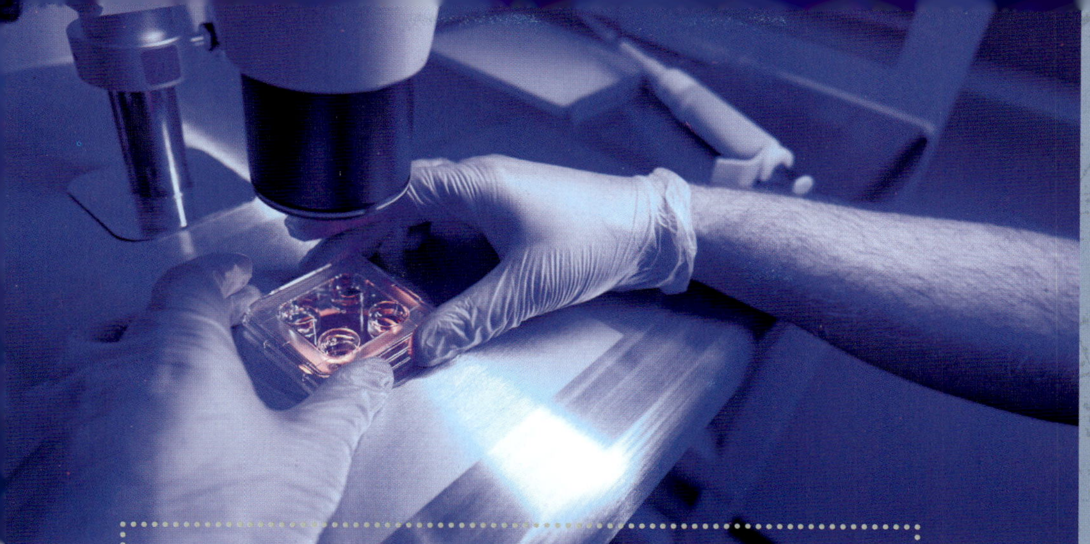

Using Stem Cells

Gene therapy is carried out in laboratories when scientists introduce viruses into special cells called stem cells. These are cells that can divide over and over. They produce not only more stem cells, but also cells that can turn into many different types of cells, such as neurons. Scientists can get stem cells from different places around the body, such as bone marrow and skin, but also from the nervous system. Once they have the cells, they add a solution containing the viruses along with chemicals to help the stem cells divide more quickly. After washing off the solutions, scientists can then inject the cells containing the normal gene into the person receiving the therapy. Once inside the body, the normal copy of the gene is passed on to other cells.

Understanding Bipolar Disorder

In 2014, scientists took samples of skin cells from people with and without bipolar disorder. They treated the cells to act like stem cells, then turn into neurons. They found that the bipolar neurons passed on signals from one to another in a more confused way than normal neurons. Scientists think this might mean that in people with bipolar disorder, genes in neurons in one part of the brain may act as though they are in another part, and neurotransmitters may then mix up messages.

From Lab to Real Life

Gene therapy is a much more complex way of treating someone with an illness than giving pills or injections. The techniques may work in a laboratory setting, but they are more difficult to predict in patients.

An Immune Response

One of the biggest challenges to gene therapy is the body's defensive shield, the immune system. It is operated by a mobile army of white blood cells that defend the body's cells when they detect attack by other organisms, such as viruses or bacteria. The viruses used in gene therapy can be recognized as intruders, too, even though they are not introducing a harmful disease.

Into Action

When the immune system goes into attack mode, the body uses up energy, which causes a person to feel exhausted. But it can also cause inflammation, or swelling, of tissue and even failure of organs such as the liver. This is why scientists work hard to find viruses that are less likely to trigger an immune response that can damage the body.

When a virus enters the body, white blood cells rush toward it to attack it. The problem with gene therapy is that if a gene-carrying virus is put inside the body, it could provoke a similar response.

Facing Facts

Many drug treatments and therapies are tested on animals such as mice to determine if they are safe for use in people. Sometimes when something works in animals, it can fail in people. For example, in the late 1950s, sleeping pills containing the drug thalidomide were tested on guinea pigs with no harmful effects. But pregnant women taking the drug unexpectedly gave birth to children with shortened limbs.

Beating the Brain Barrier

Injecting edited cells into the brain is potentially harmful, as physical damage to delicate tissues in different brain parts could affect the brain's function. Many normal medicines can be injected into the blood. They are then carried in the blood to the parts of the body that need them. But there is a barrier between blood and the brain that gene therapy transporters, such as viruses, cannot pass. Another problem is that gene therapy relies on spreading the replacement gene when cells divide and copy themselves. Neurons stop dividing in the brain shortly after birth.

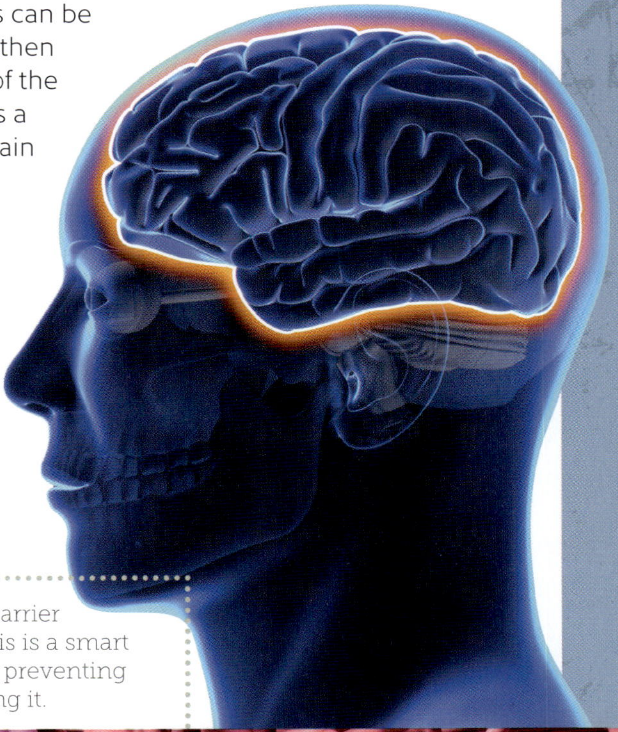

These two images illustrate the barrier between blood and the brain. This is a smart way to protect this vital organ by preventing harmful substances from reaching it.

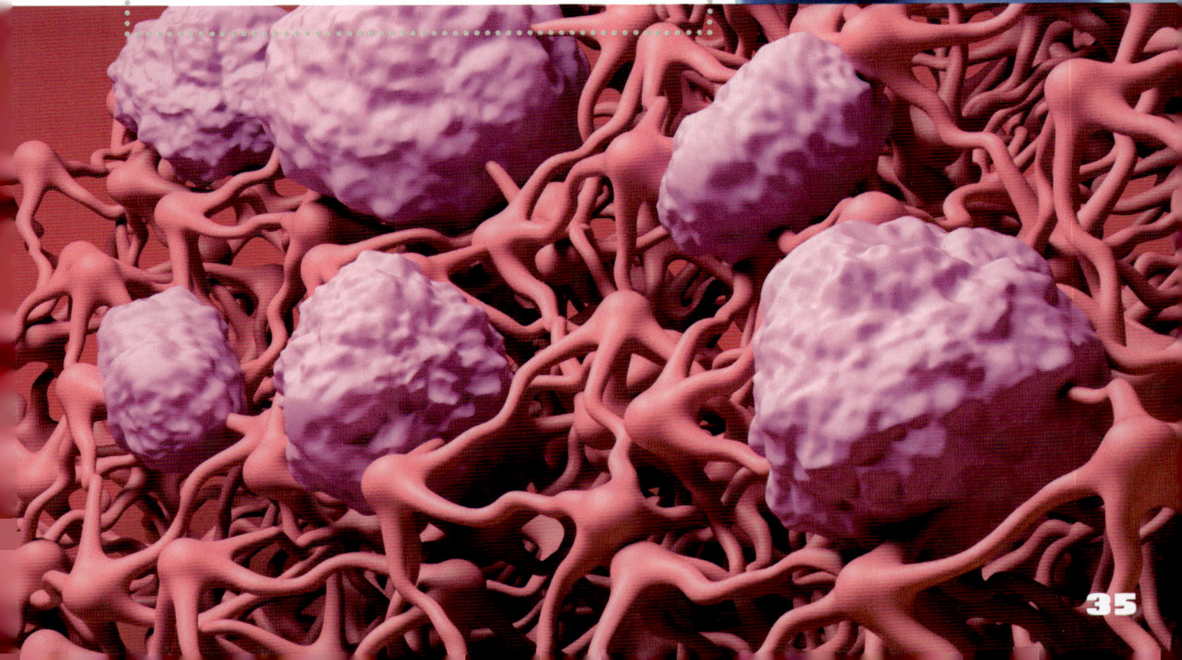

Worth the Risk?

Gene therapy is a very promising approach to dealing with many types of illness, including mental health problems. However, there are concerns about aspects of its use.

Scientists are continually researching the location and function of genes in the human genome. They are establishing how different genes work together to control how parts of the body and parts of the brain are interconnected. However, gene therapy relies on accurately delivering genes to particular places, and it is difficult to be on-target.

Triggering dangerous diseases such as leukemia is a risk when trying gene therapy.

Tools and Targeting

Sections of DNA reach specific targets using gene-editing tools. For example, one tool uses a tiny piece of DNA with a chemical code that matches that of the section of DNA sequence that needs to be edited. It binds to this section, then a protein acts like scissors to cut it out. The problem is that sometimes the tool finds and cuts out similar but not matching sections of unrelated genes. Then it might stop the other gene from working. For example, if the altered gene stops a cell from growing normally, the normal cell might turn into a cancer cell. During early attempts at SCID gene therapy, DNA missed the target and caused a type of cancer called leukemia in several patients being treated.

Many inherited illnesses affect a relatively small number of people. It is expensive to develop and use gene therapy techniques. When there are fewer users of such techniques, they remain expensive and may be unaffordable to some people desperate for gene therapy.

There are many ethical questions around gene therapy, including affordability. Is it right that therapies that could treat harmful diseases be available only in countries where people can afford them?

Understanding Bipolar Disorder

Many people are concerned about how gene therapy changes people's genomes. An improvement in one part of the genome may have unexpected and unintended consequences in other parts. For example, easing manic episodes in some people with bipolar disorder may have unexpected effects on their memory, logic, or other processes. They may not like the feel of the new personality they develop as a result of the gene therapy.

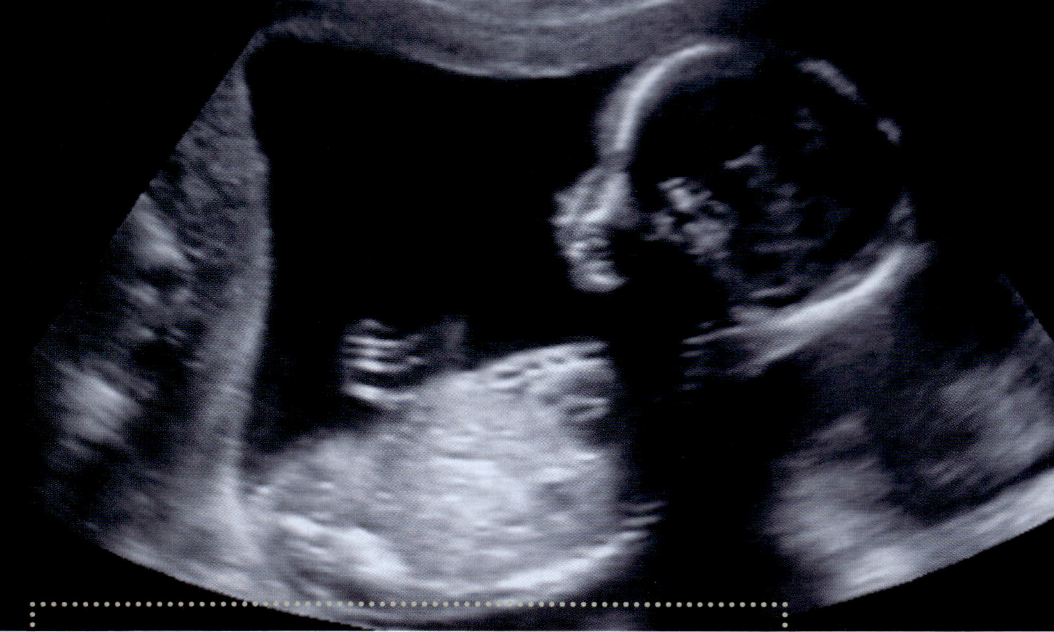

Assessing genes in babies before they are born and correcting problems could be a real possibility in the future.

Hope for Bipolar Disorder

Gene therapy for bipolar disorder will probably become a reality someday, and when it does, this development will be greeted with joy by the millions of people worldwide with the illness. Someday, it might even be possible to evaluate the genes in unborn children and use gene therapy to prevent them from getting a wide range of different diseases.

Understanding Bipolar Disorder

Gene therapy, if successful, would mean that the lives of people with bipolar disorder are not punctuated with mood episodes. It could reduce the depths and heights of mania and depression, change mania to hypomania, or even eliminate these swings altogether. It could also mean that people do not need to take medication each day to moderate their moods. People may still face the same triggers that push them along a roller coaster of emotions, but the highs and lows will not be so extreme.

Personalized Treatment

You know how some people can eat dairy foods, but others get sick if they eat milk or cheese? Everyone reacts differently to the things that go into their bodies. Many people with bipolar disorder take a wide range of antidepressants and other drugs to stabilize their moods. Some experience no side effects when taking the drugs, but others do. The tolerance they have is partly controlled by the genes in their bodies' cells. In a similar way, it is possible that gene therapy will not act in the same way for everyone because of genetic differences. That is why doctors think that personalized gene therapy is the way to go.

Before implementing gene therapy treatment, scientists and doctors will need to carry out trials to test the safety and effectiveness of gene therapy. Long-term studies on large numbers of people will give a better idea of the long-term impacts the therapy will have on health and brain function.

Editing Genes

Neurons grown from an individual's own stem cells could be tested in laboratories for tolerance to different bipolar disorder drugs so doctors know which drugs to prescribe. By editing genes in different people's neurons, scientists may be able to figure out how genes work together to control what goes on in individual brains and how to keep them healthy.

For some people, taking medication has few or no side effects, but for others the effect on their body can be far more extreme.

Help with Bipolar Disorder

Before people can get treatment or help for their bipolar disorder, they need a diagnosis. A diagnosis is when doctors or specialists examine a person and identify the symptoms, or signs, that tell them that person has a particular injury, disease, or condition.

Steps Toward Diagnosis

When someone goes to the doctor with a problem, the doctor may use special blood tests or other forms of physical examination to figure out what is wrong with the patient and give them a diagnosis. Most tests like these are not much help when it comes to diagnosing bipolar disorder. Doctors will do a physical examination, but this is to rule out illnesses or medications that might be causing a person's symptoms.

Talking It Through

To determine if someone has bipolar disorder, a doctor must talk to the patient and hear about symptoms directly from them. That's why it is very important for people to talk honestly and clearly to the doctor about their mood swings, behavior, and what life is like for them day to day.

Recording symptoms over a period of time before consultation with healthcare professionals will give them a clearer picture.

Working with Psychiatrists

A doctor who diagnoses mental health conditions such as bipolar disorder is called a psychiatrist. A psychiatrist will ask a patient about symptoms, such as mood swings, and will want to know how bad they are, how long they last, and how often they happen. They will also ask how a person feels at the time mood swings happen. Psychiatrists keep careful notes about how regularly mood swings happen. This is because one way to diagnose bipolar disorder is to see that regular episodes of high moods are often accompanied by an increase in energy, sleeplessness, and fast thinking or speech. The psychiatrist also asks people about memory, how well they find they can express themselves, and how their moods affect their relationships.

Understanding Bipolar Disorder

Before a person with bipolar disorder sees their doctor or psychiatrist, they should write down any symptoms that might help indicate depression, hypomania, or mania. It also helps if the person spends some time asking relatives about any experiences of personal mental illness, depression, or bipolar disorder. As bipolar disorder is sometimes caused in part by the genes, having a full record of any mental health problems in a family can help with a diagnosis.

"To make a diagnosis, healthcare professionals draw on information about symptoms, mood patterns, and changes in behavior."

Medication and Bipolar Disorder

After doctors identify the signs and symptoms of bipolar disorder—depression, hypomania, and mania—they can start to help a patient. In most cases, they can treat the disorder effectively and safely with medication.

Medication can help manage the symptoms of mania, such as the inability to sleep.

Treating the Symptoms

The medicines used to treat bipolar disorder cannot cure it or stop it altogether. Instead, they can reduce how bad the episodes of depression and mania feel, and they can reduce the number of times they happen. Some medications are designed to help reduce the extreme ups and downs of mood swings. These are known as mood stabilizers.

Using Antidepressants

To reduce episodes of depression, people with bipolar disorder may take antidepressants, like people with depression do. However, taking antidepressants when you have bipolar disorder can trigger an episode of hypomania, so their use is carefully monitored. Sometimes mood stabilizers will be enough to help control the depression, anyway. These medications help control and regulate neurotransmitter activity in the brain, which plays a part in controlling mood. If not, patients may also be given a medicine known as an antipsychotic to help control the depression.

Understanding Bipolar Disorder

When people are diagnosed with bipolar disorder, it is important that they are fully involved in the decisions about their treatment. This is partly because they will probably need to take medication for the rest of their lives. It's vital for them to understand that they need to keep taking the medications, even at times when they feel better.

Medication can help manage symptoms of depression.

Facing Facts

It's also important that people with bipolar disorder understand the need for patience, as it can take time to find what medications work for each individual. If one doesn't work well for them, they may have to try several others before finding the right one. After starting medication, it can also take several weeks or even months before a patient starts to feel any benefits. Some medications used to treat bipolar disorder may have possible side effects that require monitoring, such as weight gain due to changes in a person's metabolism, or how effectively they use energy from food. People may also feel drowsy or experience shaking, among other side effects. Regular checkups and monitoring of symptoms is important to make sure a person's medication is not causing further harm.

Understanding Behavior

As well as medication, sufferers of bipolar disorder can get other types of therapies to help them live as normally as they possibly can. These are often known as behavioral therapies. These usually involve talking one-to-one, with family, or in groups with people who are trained to help others deal with problems such as depression by learning techniques to cope with or control bipolar symptoms.

Identifying Patterns

The idea of cognitive behavioral therapy (CBT) is to help people identify unhealthy, negative ideas and behaviors and replace them with healthy, positive ones. CBT can help people with bipolar disorder figure out what triggers episodes and help them learn ways of coping with stress and upsetting situations.

Understanding what might cause negative ideas, such as stress at work, can help people work toward managing those thoughts.

What Is CBT?

CBT looks for practical ways to improve a person's state of mind day to day. CBT therapists help people break down overwhelming feelings into separate areas, such as situations, thoughts, emotions, physical feelings, and actions. CBT is based on the idea that these different areas are connected; the way people think about a particular situation affects how they feel about it and how they respond or act when it happens. Imagine, for example, a person who hits a problem and thinks, "I'll never be able to sort it out." This person is likely to fail and feel depressed about it. On the other hand, a person who realizes that everyone faces problems, and knows that they might be able to solve their particular problem or get help solving it, is more likely to have a positive outcome. This is an oversimplified example, but it gives you an idea of how therapists can help people look at problems in a helpful rather than unhelpful way.

Understanding Bipolar Disorder

Another example of behavioral therapy that can help people with bipolar disorder is family-focused therapy, or FFT. This therapy helps to teach patients and their families about bipolar disorder so that relatives can help patients stick with their treatment plan and recognize and manage warning signs of mood swings. FFT also helps patients and their families to identify any difficulties and conflicts within the family and show them how those problems might be causing stress for the patient and the family.

Therapists help families find ways to solve any problems or difficulties they might have, which can be a big help for patients.

Health and Bipolar Disorder

Along with experiencing the severe mood changes that bipolar disorder brings, people who have the condition may often also have physical health complications that make dealing with bipolar disorder even harder. Some of these are linked to the condition itself, and others may be a result of medication taken to try to help with symptoms or changes in lifestyle because of the difficulties of living with bipolar disorder.

People with bipolar disorder have higher rates of medical conditions compared to the general population. They can include the following.

Chronic stress: Long-term stress and mood swings in bipolar disorder can lead to high levels of cortisol, the hormone most associated with stress. Raised cortisol levels can cause problems with the immune system, inflammation, and other health complications.

Cardiovascular problems: People with bipolar disorder often have more risk of dangerous illnesses such as coronary heart disease and hypertension.

Gastrointestinal disorders: Problems with the digestive system can include irritable bowel syndrome (IBS), acid reflux, and inflammatory bowel disease (IBD).

Thyroid disorders: People may experience hypothyroidism, in which the body does not produce enough thyroid hormone, or hyperthyroidism, in which the body produces too much hormone.

Obesity: Being overweight is often linked to having bipolar disorder.

Long-term stress can cause raised cortisol levels.

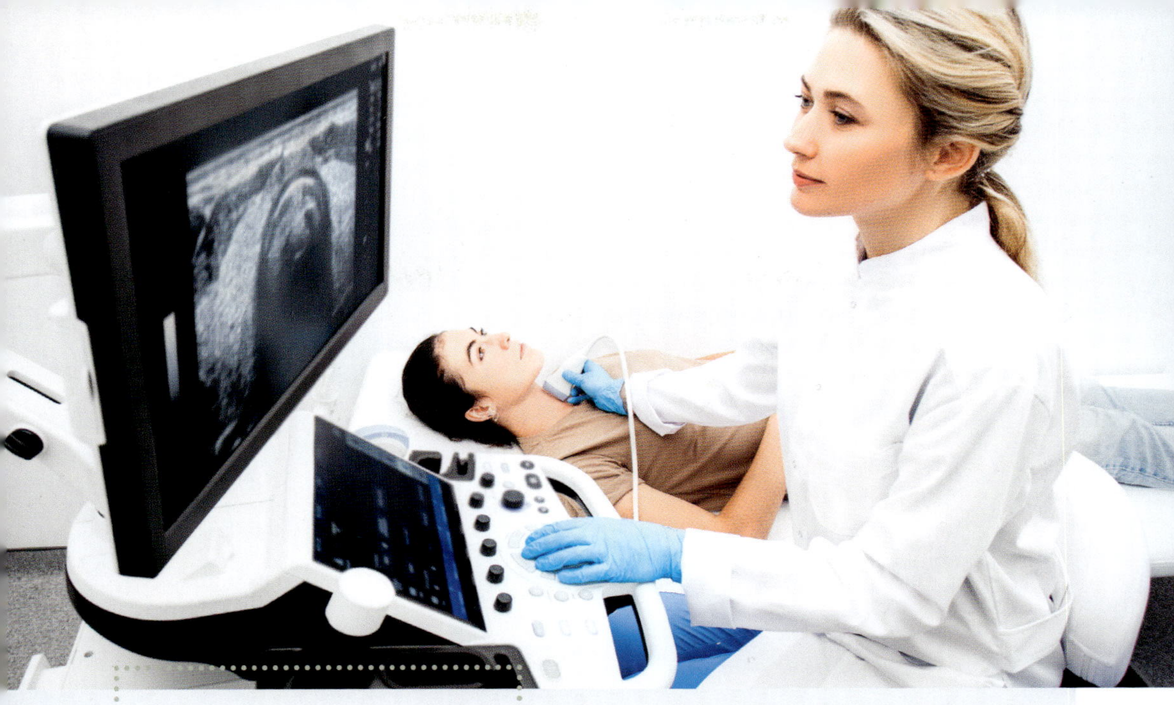

Scans may be used to check
the health of the thyroid gland.

Drugs, Alcohol, and Smoking

People with bipolar disorder are more likely than those without
the condition to turn to drugs and alcohol use as a way of dealing
with their symptoms. They are also more likely to smoke. However,
substance abuse can make symptoms worse. It often greatly
worsens mood swings and can stop medication being effective.
It also adds to physical health problems such as cardiovascular
disease, lung disease, liver disease, and many other health issues.

Dealing with Health

Although bipolar disorder brings certain medical and health complications with it, there are many things that people with the condition can do to lessen the risk of health problems. Health professionals too can play a large role in helping people who have bipolar disorder keep well.

A healthy lifestyle is one in which a person is regularly physically active, gets adequate amounts of sleep, eats healthy foods, and avoids harmful substances such as alcohol and drugs. A common side effect caused by some medications for bipolar disorder is weight gain. The medications often make people put on weight more easily, which can make people depressed and unhealthy. Eating a healthy diet can limit weight gain. If people with bipolar disorder maintain a healthy weight, it makes them feel better and, in some cases, it may even reduce their need for medication.

Eating a healthy diet and also maintaining a healthy weight are important for everyone, regardless of whether or not they have a condition such as bipolar disorder.

RESETTING THE BODY CLOCK

Scientists have discovered that people with bipolar disorder have overly sensitive body clocks, which are the timekeepers in our bodies that control circadian rhythms. Circadian rhythms tell our bodies when to sleep, wake up, and eat, and they are usually triggered by environmental stimulants, such as sunlight, darkness, and temperature. When circadian rhythms are stable, a person's mood is more stable, too. A new therapy called interpersonal and social rhythm therapy (IPSRT) helps reset the body clocks of people with bipolar disorder by establishing a daily routine of regular hours and times for sleeping, exercising, and eating. A consistent routine helps bipolar disorder sufferers manage their moods better.

THE POWER OF EXERCISE

Everyone should try to do at least 30 minutes of exercise each day. Exercise keeps people fit and makes their body release endorphins. These are feel-good chemicals that boost the mood, which is helpful in reducing the depressive symptoms of someone with bipolar disorder.

 Avoiding alcohol, drugs, and smoking can help prevent worsening symptoms and interference with medication.

 Practicing techniques such as meditation, deep-breathing exercises, yoga, or tai chi can help reduce stress, make a person more relaxed, and prevent mood triggers.

Keeping up with regular health checkups can help people keep on top of their physical and emotional health. Maintaining communication with healthcare providers makes sure that people get the best attention possible.

CHAPTER 5

Living with Bipolar Disorder

The first weeks and months after getting a diagnosis of bipolar disorder can be very difficult. People who have been told they have the condition may feel completely overwhelmed at the thought of having a lifelong illness like this. When people are getting successful medication and therapy, they start to see that although bipolar disorder will change the course of their life, it doesn't mean that they can't do the things they want to do. People can help themselves by using different coping strategies along with their medication and therapies.

Understanding Bipolar Disorder

There is no reason why having bipolar disorder should prevent most people from accomplishing their goals. People with bipolar disorder can still get married, get the job they always wanted, and lead productive and successful lives. It may just mean that they have to find different routes or take a little longer to get there. For example, many people diagnosed with bipolar disorder in their twenties continue their studies at college. They may have to take fewer classes every semester so that it takes them longer to graduate, but they still achieve a college degree in the end.

Controlling Behaviors

Having bipolar disorder is just a small part of who a person is. It does not define them. It's important for people who have bipolar disorder—and everyone else—to understand that there is a difference between the symptoms and the person.

"Symptoms will affect the behavior of a person with bipolar disorder, but people can find ways to control those behaviors, and it is not who they really are."

Finding Support

Living with bipolar disorder can be challenging, and having people to talk to can make all the difference in how a person feels and copes with their condition. Some people with bipolar disorder feel more comfortable talking to family and friends about their condition and how they are feeling about it. Other people may find it easier to join a support group. These are groups of people who all have the condition.

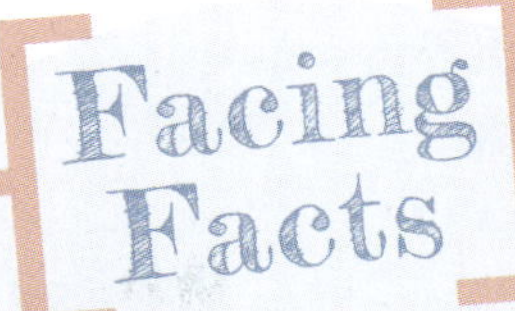

Talking to people who face many similar problems can help people realize they are not alone. It also gives people the chance to share ideas for coping and to learn from others who understand what they are going through.

Some people with bipolar disorder would like others to understand that the condition often makes people very creative and self-motivated, which helps them to be great at the jobs they choose to do.

A Plan for Living with Bipolar Disorder

One of the most important ways people with bipolar disorder can help themselves is by learning as much as they can about the condition. This can help them manage symptoms and prevent the condition from getting worse. Also, knowing what's going on can help people make sure they get the support that they need and make a plan to help themselves.

Triggering Episodes

One of the main ways people can help themselves is by learning what triggers an episode to see if they can avoid it or prepare for it better. Some people do this by keeping a chart or making notes in a journal about what they do, what happened in their day, and how they feel, as well as recording when an episode happens and how bad it is. Many people with bipolar disorder keep records like this all their lives.

Understanding Bipolar Disorder

By looking back at journal entries that cover several months, people with bipolar disorder can often see what causes triggers. Using this knowledge, they can find ways to avoid the triggers and reduce the number or severity of the episodes they have. Some people ask relatives to help them spot triggers, as the people who love them may notice that certain things, such as sudden changes in routine, can set them off. If friends and family know what a person's triggers are, they can help that person to avoid them.

Being aware that a change in seasons can affect bipolar disorder helps people plan ahead for those times.

Being Prepared

Some triggers, such as changing seasons or changes in hormonal levels, cannot really be avoided, but many can. For example, if a person you know is argumentative and shouts at you, making you stressed, you can choose to avoid that person. For triggers that cannot be avoided, at least if a person knows they are coming, they can prepare for them. For example, if being busy at work makes a person stressed, they could plan to have plenty of quiet time at home during a busy period so that things don't spiral out of control. That person can also practice ways to unwind, such as breathing exercises or listening to calming music.

Taking time out to relax during stressful times can help minimize factors that can trigger an episode.

Employment and Bipolar Disorder

The changes in mood that come with bipolar disorder can affect
a person's relationships with coworkers and employers. If a person is in
a depressive episode and is experiencing symptoms of fatigue, sadness,
and lack of interest in their work, it can be difficult for them to perform
their job well. If they become withdrawn, it can be difficult to interact with
people around them at work. At the other end of the scale, if the person
with bipolar disorder is in a manic episode, they may be very distracted,
impulsive, and take risks. That in turn makes it hard for them to carry out
tasks, and could impact how others respond to them in the workplace.

The workplace can be stressful for many people, even those without
the additional factor of a condition such as bipolar to manage.

Problems with Focus

Bipolar disorder can affect cognitive functioning, which has an impact on
how someone performs at work. They can experience issues with:

- Remembering information
- Keeping focused on a task
- Listening to instructions
- Maintaining a conversation with
  coworkers or a member of the public
- Solving problems
- Carrying out a number
  of tasks at once
- Learning new skills

It is not unusual for people with the condition to need to take time off work, sometimes for long periods. They may need to go to the hospital to have treatment, or feel unable to work due to episodes that make normal activities feel impossible. Being absent from work for extended periods can lead to a buildup of work, which can add to the already-intense pressure and stress of living with bipolar disorder. And unless someone works in a supportive workplace, resentment from coworkers who may have to shoulder some of their workload can also add to the problem.

Problems with Sharing

Changing job can also be hard for people with bipolar disorder. Gaps in employment due to illness can be difficult to explain if potential employers are not aware of the condition or do not understand it. Often, people with the condition may not want to share that they have bipolar disorder with people they do not know well. That can make changing career or going back to work in a new job role after a period of time away very challenging.

Applying for new jobs or seeking out promotions may be difficult for someone with bipolar disorder. Simply keeping a job may be challenging due to the unpredictable nature of the condition.

Dealing with Employment

Having a job that can accommodate the needs of someone with bipolar disorder can help them better manage it—going to work can be very positive for people and enrich their lives if the workplace they are in can support their needs. While traditionally many people with bipolar disorder have found it difficult to find and maintain employment that suits them, today, finding and keeping a job that can accommodate their needs is becoming much easier. That is thanks to changing attitudes within the workplace, and society at large.

TALKING ABOUT IT

Having honest, open discussions about conditions such as bipolar disorder within workplaces encourages people with the condition to feel that they can share their diagnosis with employers and coworkers. By breaking down stigmas and misconceptions surrounding the condition, people can be more understanding of those who experience it. A supportive environment in which people are empathic to others with mental health conditions helps those with bipolar disorder go to work and keep their jobs.

A FLEXIBLE JOB

Flexible schedules such as adjusted hours, working from home, part-time working, or job sharing can all help a person continue to work. With flexibility, they can better manage changes in mood and energy levels. It also gives them the time needed to go for treatment or check in with healthcare professionals to make sure their treatment plans are working. Being able to take breaks as needed at work also helps people better manage their symptoms.

A structured and predictable work routine with clear expectations and deadlines can help people manage their time and keep organized. A stable routine also helps to reduce anxiety at work, because people know what to expect and when.

Today, a number of organizations actively encourage self-care at work, giving people time to take breaks or take part in stress-reducing activities such as yoga classes.

Having regular check-ins with supervisors to discuss workload and make any adjustments needed helps people feel that they can talk about difficulties and make changes that can help them continue with their job.

More than ever, employers today are recognizing that a healthy work environment creates healthy, happy workers—and that is good for business.

Bipolar Disorder and the Future

In the past, people with bipolar disorder were often considered insane. For example, in nineteenth-century France, the term "circular insanity" was sometimes used. People with the illness were sometimes locked away or punished to stop the symptoms. Thankfully, today, bipolar disorder is much more widely known, better understood, and properly treated.

Research Continues

Scientists are busy pinpointing the genes responsible for the disorder and honing techniques of gene editing for possible gene therapy in the future. Doctors are becoming better at diagnosing the illness and devising better drug treatments. Educators are spreading the word about what it means to have and live with bipolar disorder.

Managing Bipolar Disorder

People with bipolar disorder are now equipped with a toolbox of different ways to deal with their episodes. They can use a range of techniques to ease the depths and heights of mood swings by identifying and controlling their triggers. People can choose from a range of drug treatments and therapies to ease symptoms during episodes.

Less Stigma and Better Understanding

There is also much less stigma about having bipolar disorder nowadays—after all, why should anyone feel ashamed of an inherited illness? This situation has been helped by several celebrities, including the late actress Carrie Fisher and singer Demi Lovato, talking openly about having bipolar disorder. People with the condition are now often treated with greater compassion and understanding.

Today, more group support is available for people, sometimes online, where individuals can share their experiences.

Understanding Bipolar Disorder

To have episodes of mania and depression during your life is unusual. It can be frightening to witness and live through, but it does not make a person abnormal. Everyone is different and has different thoughts and reactions to anyone else.

Thankfully today, people are better informed than ever about mental health and conditions such as bipolar disorder. With continued improved education, medical help, and a more tolerant, inclusive society, the outlook for people with the disorder looks brighter than ever.

"Mental illness such as bipolar disorder can be treated and people with the condition can live fulfilling lives."

Glossary

academic relating to education such as schoolwork

acid reflux a condition in which stomach acid flows back into the esophagus (the tube that connects the stomach to the mouth), causing symptoms such as heartburn

agitated on edge and irritable

antidepressants medications prescribed to treat depression

argumentative entering easily into arguments

attention deficit hyperactivity disorder (ADHD) a disorder characterized by symptoms such as problems with focus and attention, extreme energy, and impulsive behavior

bacteria tiny organisms that can cause infections or diseases

barrier something that prevents movement from one place to another

bone marrow soft tissue found in the center of bones

cardiovascular disease a group of disorders that affect the heart and blood vessels, including heart disease and strokes

chromosomes threadlike structures found in cells that carry genetic information

chronic long-lasting or persistent

circulates moves around

cognitive relating to thought, memory, or understanding

coping strategies ways of dealing with difficulties

coronary heart disease a condition characterized by a narrowing or blockage of the coronary arteries, leading to reduced blood flow to the heart muscle

define to explain or make clear

devising creating a plan

discrimination unfair treatment or prejudice toward a person or a group of people based on certain characteristics, such as race, gender, age, disability, or religion

distorted altered so that it does not represent a true image

distracted unable to focus on something

drowsy sleepy, not alert

elated extremely happy

eliminate to get rid of something

empathy the ability to understand and share the feelings, thoughts, and experiences of others

ethical relating to values that are considered important, such as fairness and equality

evaluate to assess or judge something

expectations standards and outcomes that are assumed will be achieved

extracurricular activities undertaken outside of regular academic or work responsibilities, such as sports, clubs, hobbies, and volunteer work

honing making better or improving

host cell a cell that provides a suitable environment for the survival of another organism

hypertension high blood pressure

inappropriate not accepted behavior

inflammatory bowel disease (IBD) a group of conditions in which the bowel is inflamed, including Crohn's disease and ulcerative colitis

insane considered extremely mentally ill

interacting communicating verbally or nonverbally with others

invade to enter something with the potential to do harm

irritable bowel syndrome (IBS) a common gastrointestinal disorder characterized by abdominal pain, bloating, and diarrhea or constipation

isolate to separate or disconnect
from others

logical related to reasoning and
thought processes mostly
unaffected by emotion and
often used to solve problems
or make decisions

mentor a trusted person who
provides guidance and help

misconceptions views and beliefs
based on facts that may not
be true

mobile able to easily move around

moderate to control and keep
in balance

monitored checked the
progression of something

motivated encouraged

mucus a slimy substance

mutations permanent changes
in the DNA sequence of a gene

outspoken describes a person who
easily shares thoughts verbally

overwhelmed feeling unable
to cope

personalized designed or changed
to suit a particular person

predict to estimate the likelihood
of something happening

prescribe to recommend particular
treatment such as medication

psychiatric related to the
diagnosis, study, and treatment
of mental disorders

punctuated broken up into
sections

rejection refusal to accept
something or someone

retain to keep hold of

schizophrenia a severe mental
disorder characterized by
disturbing thoughts, emotions,
and behavior

segments pieces of something

self-esteem confidence in one's
own worth or abilities

social cues nonverbal signs
given by other people in
social situations, such as facial
expressions and body movements

stigma a negative attitude, belief, or
perception toward a person based
on their characteristics

thyroid a gland in a person's neck,
which controls many parts of
their body from temperature
to energy levels

tolerance the ability to accept
and accommodate things

tuition teaching

unrelated not connected
to something

unstable not mentally healthy

withdrawn avoiding social contact

witness to observe something
firsthand

Books

Mental Health America. *Where to Start: A Survival Guide to Anxiety, Depression, and Other Mental Health Challenges.* Rocky Pond Books, 2023.

Rosenthal, Sandra J. *I'm a Quantum Dot Chemist Now!* WS Education, 2023.

Smith, Hilary T. *Welcome to the Jungle: Facing Bipolar Without Freaking Out.* Conari Press, 2024.

Websites

Understand bipolar disorder by visiting:
https://kidshealth.org/en/teens/bipolar.html

Get answers to all your questions about bipolar disorder at:
www.camh.ca/en/health-info/guides-and-publications/when-a-parent-has-bipolar-disorder

Find out more about coping with bipolar disorder at:
www.nampaimagine.com/mental-health-blog/5-coping-skills-for-teenage-bipolar-disorder

Publisher's note to educators and parents:
All the websites featured above have been carefully reviewed to ensure that they are suitable for students. However, many websites change often, and we cannot guarantee that a site's future contents will continue to meet our high standards of educational value. Please be advised that students should be closely monitored whenever they access the Internet.

Index

About the Author

Sarah Eason has written many books for children and young adults. Researching and writing this book has highlighted the complexities of bipolar disorder, from its causes to management, and the challenges that people with the condition face. She hopes this book is an informative, helpful, and compassionate resource for readers interested in the topic or affected by it.